First World War
and Army of Occupation
War Diary
France, Belgium and Germany

36 DIVISION
107 Infantry Brigade
Royal Irish Rifles
10th Battalion
3 October 1915 - 19 January 1918

WO95/2503/4

The Naval & Military Press Ltd
www.nmarchive.com
Published in association with The National Archives

Published by

The Naval & Military Press Ltd

Unit 10 Ridgewood Industrial Park,

Uckfield, East Sussex,

TN22 5QE England

Tel: +44 (0) 1825 749494

www.naval-military-press.com

www.nmarchive.com

This diary has been reprinted in facsimile from the original. Any imperfections are inevitably reproduced and the quality may fall short of modern type and cartographic standards.

© Crown Copyright
Images reproduced by permission of The National Archives, London, England, 2015.

Contents

Document type	Place/Title	Date From	Date To
Heading	WO95/2503/4 10 Battalion Royal Irish Rifles		
Heading	36th Division 107th Infy Bde 10th Bn Roy. Irish Rif. 1915 Oct-Dec 1917		
War Diary	Folkestone	03/10/1915	03/10/1915
War Diary	Boulogne	04/10/1915	04/10/1915
War Diary	Flesselles	05/10/1915	05/10/1915
War Diary	Puchevillers	09/10/1915	09/10/1915
War Diary	Couin	10/10/1915	10/10/1915
War Diary	Hebuterne	11/10/1915	11/10/1915
War Diary	Couin	17/10/1915	17/10/1915
War Diary	Vignacourt	19/10/1915	19/10/1915
War Diary	Berteaucourt	22/10/1915	22/10/1915
Heading	36 Div 107 Bde 4th Division War Diaries 10th Battn. Royal Irish Rifles Oct November To January 1915-16		
Heading	107th Inf Bde. 4th Division. 10th Battn Royal Irish Rifles. November 1915		
War Diary	Berteaucourt	04/11/1915	04/11/1915
War Diary	Puchevillers	04/11/1915	04/11/1915
War Diary	Beausart	05/11/1915	05/11/1915
War Diary	Forceville	14/11/1915	14/11/1915
War Diary	In Trenches Sector 75-85	14/11/1915	14/11/1915
War Diary	Varennes	26/11/1915	26/11/1915
Heading	107th Inf Bde. 4th Division. 10th Battn Royal Irish Rifles. December 1915		
War Diary	Varennes	01/12/1915	01/12/1915
War Diary	In Trenches	02/12/1915	08/12/1915
War Diary	Acheux	08/12/1915	08/12/1915
War Diary	In Trenches	13/12/1915	17/12/1915
War Diary	Mailly-Maillet	17/12/1915	17/12/1915
War Diary	In Trenches	21/12/1915	25/12/1915
War Diary	Acheux	25/12/1915	25/12/1915
War Diary	In Trenches	29/12/1915	01/01/1916
Heading	107th Inf Bde. 4th Division. 10th Battn Royal Irish Rifles January 1916		
War Diary	Mailly-Maillet	01/01/1916	03/01/1916
War Diary	Trenches	03/01/1916	07/01/1916
War Diary	Varennes	07/01/1916	11/01/1916
War Diary	Trenches	11/01/1916	15/01/1916
War Diary	Mailly-Maillet	15/01/1916	19/01/1916
War Diary	Trenches	19/01/1916	23/01/1916
War Diary	Varennes	23/01/1916	27/01/1916
War Diary	Trenches	27/01/1916	31/01/1916
War Diary	Mailly Maillet	01/02/1916	04/02/1916
War Diary	In Trenches	04/02/1916	08/02/1916
War Diary	Mailly Maillet	08/02/1916	12/02/1916
War Diary	In Trenches	12/02/1916	16/02/1916
War Diary	Mailly Maillet	16/02/1916	20/02/1916
War Diary	In Trenches	20/02/1916	24/02/1916
War Diary	Varennes	24/02/1916	28/02/1916
War Diary	In Trenches	03/03/1916	07/03/1916

Type	Location	From	To
War Diary	Mailly-Maillet	07/03/1916	11/03/1916
War Diary	In Trenches	11/03/1916	15/03/1916
War Diary	Mailly-Maillet	15/03/1916	21/03/1916
War Diary	In Trenches	21/03/1916	27/03/1916
War Diary	Mailly-Maillet	27/03/1916	28/03/1916
War Diary	Lealvillers	28/03/1916	08/05/1916
War Diary	Martinsart	08/05/1916	30/05/1916
War Diary	In Trenches	30/05/1916	31/05/1916
Heading	107th Brigade 36th Division. 1/10th Battalion Royal Irish Rifles. June 1916		
Miscellaneous	A Form Messages And Signals		
War Diary	In Trenches	07/06/1916	07/06/1916
War Diary	Mesnil	07/06/1916	13/06/1916
War Diary	In Trenches	13/06/1916	20/06/1916
War Diary	Lealvillers	23/06/1916	23/06/1916
War Diary	Forceville	27/06/1916	27/06/1916
War Diary	Lealvillers	28/06/1916	28/06/1916
War Diary	Aveluy, Wood	30/06/1916	30/06/1916
War Diary		03/06/1916	03/06/1916
Heading	107th Brigade. 36th Division. 1/10th Battalion Royal Irish Rifles July 1916		
War Diary	Speyside Thiepval Wood	01/07/1916	01/07/1916
War Diary	Ross Castle	01/07/1916	01/07/1916
War Diary		02/07/1916	02/07/1916
War Diary	Thiepval Wood	02/07/1916	02/07/1916
War Diary		01/07/1916	01/07/1916
War Diary	Thiepval Wood	02/07/1916	02/07/1916
War Diary	Martinsart	04/07/1916	04/07/1916
War Diary	Harponville	05/07/1916	11/07/1916
War Diary	Auxi-Le Chateaux	11/07/1916	31/07/1916
War Diary		04/07/1916	25/07/1916
War Diary	La Plus Douve Fm	01/08/1916	01/08/1916
War Diary	Near Eglise Neuve	05/08/1916	17/08/1916
War Diary	St Quentin Cabaret	24/08/1916	27/08/1916
War Diary	Trenches	01/09/1916	23/09/1916
War Diary	Trenches	12/09/1916	29/09/1916
War Diary	Neuve Eglise	27/09/1916	23/10/1916
War Diary		11/10/1916	31/10/1916
War Diary	Neuve Eglise	04/11/1916	16/11/1916
War Diary		15/11/1916	28/11/1916
War Diary	On Service	01/11/1916	28/12/1916
War Diary		02/12/1916	13/12/1916
War Diary		12/12/1916	30/12/1916
War Diary	On Service	05/12/1916	22/12/1916
War Diary	In The Field	03/01/1917	27/01/1917
War Diary		03/01/1917	16/01/1917
War Diary	In The Field	17/01/1917	28/01/1917
War Diary		16/01/1917	16/01/1917
War Diary	Neuve Eglise Bulford Camp	04/02/1917	19/02/1917
War Diary	Pinchboom	26/02/1917	26/02/1917
War Diary	Redlodge	27/02/1917	27/02/1917
War Diary	La Douve Sector	01/03/1917	07/03/1917
War Diary	Redlodge	09/03/1917	12/03/1917
War Diary	Kemmel Sector	13/03/1917	19/03/1917
War Diary	Derry Huts	19/03/1917	24/03/1917
War Diary	Kemmel Sector	25/03/1917	31/03/1917

War Diary	Kemmel	01/04/1917	07/04/1917
War Diary	Wakefield Huts	08/04/1917	15/04/1917
War Diary	Hazebrouck	16/04/1917	16/04/1917
War Diary	Arques	17/04/1917	17/04/1917
War Diary	Moringhem	22/04/1917	30/04/1917
War Diary	Arques	01/05/1917	01/05/1917
War Diary	Hazebrouck	02/05/1917	02/05/1917
War Diary	Meteren	03/05/1917	14/05/1917
War Diary	Hille	16/05/1917	30/05/1917
War Diary	Berthen	01/06/1917	06/06/1917
War Diary	Messines Wytschaete Ridge	07/06/1917	07/06/1917
War Diary	Hille	09/06/1917	13/06/1917
War Diary	Bailleul	18/06/1917	18/06/1917
War Diary	Wytschaete	19/06/1917	21/06/1917
War Diary	Oost Averne	24/06/1917	24/06/1917
War Diary		22/06/1917	25/06/1917
War Diary	Oost Averne	26/06/1917	28/06/1917
War Diary	Locre	30/06/1917	30/06/1917
War Diary	Opposite Messines Riage	07/06/1917	07/06/1917
War Diary	Outtersteen	01/07/1917	05/07/1917
War Diary	Caestre	06/07/1917	06/07/1917
War Diary	Renescure	07/07/1917	07/07/1917
War Diary	Le Poovre	08/07/1917	20/07/1917
War Diary	Le Poovre	16/07/1917	16/07/1917
War Diary	Esquerdes	25/07/1917	25/07/1917
War Diary	Oudezeele	26/07/1917	31/07/1917
War Diary	Watou	02/08/1917	02/08/1917
War Diary	Plum Fm	05/08/1917	05/08/1917
War Diary	Llhlan Fm	06/08/1917	07/08/1917
War Diary	Vlamertinghe	12/08/1917	12/08/1917
War Diary	Plum Fm	14/08/1917	14/08/1917
War Diary	Vlamertinghe	16/08/1917	16/08/1917
War Diary	Vinery	18/08/1917	18/08/1917
War Diary	Vlamertinghe	20/08/1917	20/08/1917
War Diary	Oudezeele	24/08/1917	24/08/1917
War Diary	Barastre	27/08/1917	27/08/1917
War Diary	Ytres	28/08/1917	31/08/1917
War Diary	Trescault Sector	03/09/1917	03/09/1917
War Diary	Equancourt	08/09/1917	09/09/1917
War Diary	Trescault	15/09/1917	15/09/1917
War Diary	Metz	20/09/1917	21/09/1917
War Diary	Trescault	26/09/1917	27/09/1917
War Diary	Equancourt	30/09/1917	29/10/1917
War Diary		01/10/1917	31/10/1917
War Diary	Havrincourt Sector	02/11/1917	30/11/1917
War Diary	Berneville	01/12/1917	27/12/1917
War Diary	Laneuville (Corbie)	01/01/1918	07/01/1918
War Diary	Mesnil S.N	11/01/1918	11/01/1918
War Diary	Dury	12/01/1918	12/01/1918
War Diary	Grugies	18/01/1918	22/01/1918
War Diary	Fontaine Le Clerques	23/01/1918	30/01/1918
War Diary		04/01/1918	19/01/1918

WO95/2503/4
10 Battalion Royal Irish Rifles

36TH DIVISION
107TH INFY BDE

10TH BN ROY. IRISH RIF.
~~OCT 1915 &~~
1915 OCT ~~FEB 1916~~ - DEC 1917

DISBANDED

Army Form C. 2118

10th (S) Bn ROYAL IRISH RIFLES

WAR DIARY or INTELLIGENCE SUMMARY

(Erase heading not required.)

Secret

Instructions regarding War Diaries and Intelligence Summaries are contained in F.S. Regs., Part II. and the Staff Manual respectively. Title Pages will be prepared in manuscript.

Place	Date	Hour	Summary of Events and Information	Remarks and references to Appendices
FOLKESTONE	3/10/15	10 p.m.	Sailed for FRANCE.	
BOULOGNE	4/10/15	1 a.m.	Arrived	
"	4/10/15	11 p.m.	Entrained	
FLESSELLES	5/10/15	5 a.m.	Detrained and marched to VIGNACOURT	
PUCHEVILLERS	9/10/15		By route march on the way to the trenches of the 48th Division	
COUIN	10/10/15		" " "	
HEBUTERNE	11/10/15		" " "	
"			Did trench duty from 11/10/15 till 17/10/15 with the 48th Division	
COUIN	17/10/15		Arrived & marched on the 18/10/15 to PUCHEVILLERS.	
VIGNACOURT	19/10/15		Arrived and marched on the 22nd Oct. to BERTEAUCOURT.	
BERTEAUCOURT	22/10/15		Arrived & went into billets	

H. Fennell Col
Comdg 10th R. Irish Rifles

36 DIV
107 BDE

Attached 4th Division
War Diaries
10th Battn. Royal Irish Rifles

Oct November, To January
1915 - 16

107th Inf Bde.
4th Division,

10th Battn ROYAL IRISH RIFLES.

NOVEMBER 1915

10th Bn Royal Irish Rifles

WAR DIARY
or
INTELLIGENCE SUMMARY
(Erase heading not required.)

Army Form C. 2118

Secret

Place	Date	Hour	Summary of Events and Information	Remarks and references to Appendices
BERTEAUCOURT	4/11/15	10 a.m.	marched out - to form the 4th Division	
PUCHEVILLERS	4/11/15		arrived & marched on 5/11/15	
BEAUSART	5/11/15		arrived & marched into the trenches on the 7/11/15. Formed Brigade Reserve in MAILLY-MAILLET	
FORCEVILLE	14/11/15		marched & went billets & proceeded to the trenches again on 20/11/15 relieving the 1st Royal Warwickshire Regt.	
IN Trenches Section 75-85	20/11/15 to 26/11/15		The 1st Rifle Brigade and 1st R. Irish Fusiliers were North & South of the line of trenches respectively. Marched to billets on 26/11/15	
VARENNES	26/11/15		In rest billets until 2/12/15	

H Kennard
Col
Comdg 10th Royal Irish Rifles

107th Inf Bde.

4th Division.

10th Battn ROYAL IRISH RIFLES.

DECEMBER 1915

10th Bn Royal Irish Rifles

Army Form C. 2118

WAR DIARY or INTELLIGENCE SUMMARY
(Erase heading not required.)

Secret

Place	Date	Hour	Summary of Events and Information	Remarks and references to Appendices
VARENNES In Trenches	1/12/15 2/12/15 to 8/12/15		In rest Billets. Marched to trenches to relieve 1st Royal Warwickshire Regt - Sectors 75 & 85 inclusive 1st Rifle Brigade on the left and 1st Royal Irish Fusiliers on the Right of the P.P.R.	
ACHEUX In Trenches	8/12/15 13/12/15 to 17/12/15	11 am.	Arrived in rest-billets & marched to trenches on 13/12/15. Marched to trenches & relieved 1st Royal Warwickshire Regt - Sectors 75 & 85 inclusive 1st Rifle Brigade on the left and 1st Royal Irish Fusiliers on the right of the P.P.R. Capt. C. W. Griffith wounded in the thigh on 14/12/15.	
MAILLY MAILLET In Trenches	17/12/15 24/12/15 to 25/12/15	11 pm	Marched to rest-billets. Returned to trenches & relieved 1st R. Warwickshire Regt in sectors 75 - 85 inclusive 15th Royal Irish Rifles on the left and 9th Royal Irish Rifles on the right of the P.P.R.	
ACHEUX In Trenches	25/12/15 29/12/15 to 1/1/16	12 pm.	Arrived in rest billets & marched to trenches on 29/12/15. Marched to trenches & relieved 1st R. Warwickshire Regt in Sectors 75 & 85 inclusive 15th Royal Irish Rifles on the left and 9th Royal Irish Rifles on the right of the P.P.R.	

M Kennard Col
Comdg 10th Royal Irish Rifles

107th Inf Bde.

4th Division.

10th Battn ROYAL IRISH RIFLES

J A N U A R Y   1 9 1 6

Army Form C. 2118

WAR DIARY
or for January 1916
INTELLIGENCE SUMMARY 10th Bn Royal Irish Rifles
(5)
(Erase heading not required.)

Instructions regarding War Diaries and Intelligence Summaries are contained in F. S. Regs., Part II. and the Staff Manual respectively. Title Pages will be prepared in manuscript.

Place	Date	Hour	Summary of Events and Information	Remarks and references to Appendices
MAILLY-MAILLET	1-1-16 / 2-1-16		In billets.	
Trenches	3-1-16 / 6-1-16		Relieved 8th Br Royal Irish Rifles in trenches sectors S3 to 63 opposite with infantry	
	7-1-16		AUCHONVILLERS.	
VARENNES	7-1-16 / 11-1-16		In rest-billets.	
Trenches	11-1-16 / 15-1-16		Relieved 8th Br Royal Irish Rifles opposite with front of AUCHONVILLERS.	
MAILLY-MAILLET	15-1-16 / 18-1-16		In rest Billets. On the night of the 17th the Bn dug a new trench about 600 x long & advanced our front line about 90x. The 8th R.I. Rifles put up the wire in front.	
Trenches	18-1-16 / 22-1-16		Relieved 8th Br Royal Irish Rifles in front of AUCHONVILLERS.	
VARENNES	23-1-16 / 27-1-16		In rest Billets.	
Trenches	27-1-16 / 31-1-16		Relieved 8th Br Royal Irish Rifles in front of AUCHONVILLERS.	

W. Ormsby
Major for Col
Comdg 10th R Irish Rifles

Army Form C. 2118

WAR DIARY
or
INTELLIGENCE SUMMARY
(Erase heading not required.)

February 1916 period

10th (S) Bn Royal Irish Rifles

Instructions regarding War Diaries and Intelligence Summaries are contained in F.S. Regs., Part II. and the Staff Manual respectively. Title Pages will be prepared in manuscript.

Place	Date	Hour	Summary of Events and Information	Remarks and references to Appendices
MAILLY MAILLET	1-2-16 to 4-2-16		In rest billets	
In trenches	4-2-16 to 8-2-16		In front of AUCHONVILLERS relieving the 8th Bn Royal Irish Rifles	
MAILLY MAILLET	8-2-16 to 12-2-16		In rest billets	
In Trenches	12-2-16 to 16-2-16		Relieved 8th Bn Royal Irish Rifles in trenches in front of AUCHONVILLERS. The following detachments being attached to the Bn for instruction: 2 platoons 14th R.I. Rifles, 2 platoons 9th R. Innis. Fus., 2 platoons 11th R. Innis. Fus.	
MAILLY MAILLET	16-2-16 to 20-2-16		In rest billets	
In trenches	20-2-16 to 24-2-16		Relieved 8th Bn Royal Irish Rifles in trenches in front of AUCHONVILLERS. The following were attached to the Bn for instruction for period 20-2-16 to 22-2-16 : - 1 Coy 14th R.I. Rfs, 2 platoons 9th R. Innis. Fus. The Bn was relieved by the 9th R.I. Innis. Fus on 24-2-16.	
VARENNES	24-2-16 to end of February		In rest billets	

B. Woodwin
Major
Lt Col Royal Irish Rifles

Confidential

Army Form C. 2118

WAR DIARY or INTELLIGENCE SUMMARY

(Erase heading not required.)

March 1916 10th Bn. Royal Irish Rifles

Instructions regarding War Diaries and Intelligence Summaries are contained in F. S. Regs., Part II. and the Staff Manual respectively. Title Pages will be prepared in manuscript.

Place	Date	Hour	Summary of Events and Information	Remarks and references to Appendices
In Trenches	3/3/16 to 3/3/16		Marched from rest billets at VARENNES to trenches & relieved 7th R.I. Rifles in trenches opposite AUCHONVILLERS. Lieut. Duck wounded on 6th by shrapnel	
MAILLY-MAILLET	7/3/16 to 11/3/16		Relieved by 8th Bn R.Irish Rifles in trenches — rest billets	
In Trenches	12/3/16 to 15/3/16		Relieved 8th R. Irish Rifles in Trenches opposite AUCHONVILLERS	
MAILLY-MAILLET	16/3/16 to 19/3/16		In rest billets	
In Trenches	20/3/16 to 25/3/16		Relieved 8th Bn R.Irish Rifles in trenches opposite AUCHONVILLERS	
MAILLY-MAILLET	21/3/16 to 25/3/16		In rest billets	
LEALVILLERS	26/3/16		Marched to rest billets at LEALVILLERS	

W.H. Dunn
Major Comdg
10th R. Irish Rifles

WAR DIARY or INTELLIGENCE SUMMARY

Army Form C. 2118

Vol 7
XXXVI
April 1916
10th Bn Royal Irish Rifles

Place	Date	Hour	Summary of Events and Information	Remarks and references to Appendices
LEALVILLERS	from 1/4/16 to 30/4/16		In rest billets.	

C.H. Goodwin
Major
Comdg 10th R. Irish Rifles

Original
Month of May 1916   Vol 8   Army Form C. 2118
                                    10th Bn Royal Irish Rifles

WAR DIARY
or
INTELLIGENCE SUMMARY
(Erase heading not required.)

Place	Date	Hour	Summary of Events and Information	Remarks and references to Appendices
LEALVILLERS	1-5-16 to 8-5-16		Bn rest billets.	
MARTINSART	8-5-16 to 30-5-16		The Bn moved to MARTINSART to relieve the 14/R.Ir. Rifles and found working parties in the THIEPVAL trench sector. One Company (C) was at HESNIL.	
In trenches	30-5-16		The Bn moved to the trenches opposite HAMEL in the totals 12th Bn Royal Irish Rifles	
	31-5-16	all day	The Bn relieved the [struck] 12th Bn Royal Irish Rifles. The Bn was heavily shelled and trench damaged during the 31st and suffered a few casualties.	

R.H. Goodwin
Lt Col
Comdg 10th R. Irish Rifles

107th Brigade
36th Division.

1/10th BATTALION

ROYAL IRISH RIFLES.

JUNE 1916

"A" Form. Army Form C. 2121.
MESSAGES AND SIGNALS.

TO: A.G.'s Office Base

Day of Month: 6/7/16

AAA

Herewith W.ar Diary for the
[smith] of June 1916

[signature] Major
Comdg 10th B. [?] Rifles

Army Form C. 2118

WAR DIARY 10/n6 ~~xxxvi.~~ Original 10. R. Irish Rif.
or
INTELLIGENCE SUMMARY

(Erase heading not required.)

for June 1916

Instructions regarding War Diaries and Intelligence Summaries are contained in F. S. Regs., Part II. and the Staff Manual respectively. Title Pages will be prepared in manuscript.

Vol 9

Place	Date	Hour	Summary of Events and Information	Remarks and references to Appendices
In Trenches	up to 7-6-16		Relieved in HAMEL sector by 15th R.I. Rifles + moved to billets	
MESNIL	7-6-16 to 13-6-16		In MESNIL in billets	
In Trenches	13-6-16 to 20-6-16		Relieved the 15th R.I. Rifles in H A M E S sector + moved to in AVELUY WOOD	
LEALVILLERS	23-6-16		By route march to billets	
FORCEVILLE	27-6-16		" " " "	
LEALVILLERS	28-6-16		" " " "	
AVELUY WOOD	30-6-16		Marched to lit-trenches prior to attack to take place on 1st July.	
	3.6.16		The following awards + mentions appeared in Sir D. Haig's dispatch.	
			No 14487 Sergt (acts. Sergt. Major) John Dale — Military Medal	
			" 14967 Rifleman ~~Robert~~ H. a. C. Newport — Military Medal	
			Col H.C. Bernard — Mention	
			Major W.R. Goodwin — Mention	

R.H. Goodwin
Major 10th R.I. Rifles

107th Brigade,
36th Division.

1/10th BATTALION

ROYAL IRISH RIFLES.

JULY 1916

36 107/36 July
10 R I R
10 R172
10 R I Rifles

WAR DIARY
INTELLIGENCE SUMMARY

Army Form C. 2118.

Vol 10

Hour, Date, Place	Summary of Events and Information	Remarks and references to Appendices
6 a.m. 1 July 1916 SPEYSIDE, THIEPVAL WOOD	Battalion formed up prior to moving up for the attack	
6.53 a.m.	Battalion moved off. Coming under Machine Gun fire from THIEPVAL VILLAGE a few minutes later.	
ROSS CASTLE 7.10 a.m.		
7.45 a.m.	The Commanding Officer Colonel H C BERNARD was killed by a shell. The Battalion continued to advance though suffering heavily from shell & Machine Gun fire the ground being much cut up & difficult to cross. The Battalion went over our own front line trenches & formed up in NO MANS LAND in artillery formation in support of 109th & 108th Bdes.	
8 a.m.	By this time many of the Officers & Senior NCO's had been hit. Up to this point Captain J E SUGDEN (Adjutant) had commanded the Battalion. At 10.30 a.m. MAJOR W. R. GOODWIN assumed command of the Battalion. The Battalion commenced to advance to the attack over the open ground under heavy enfilade fire (Machine Guns) from THIEPVAL VILLAGE. The Battalion reached German support line. After this the Battalion became much cut up. The units x as worth the Officers & NCO's were killed very few reports were sent in.	
12.30 p.m.		
5.30 p.m.	"D" Company reports to be in German 3rd line & sent for more ammunition. MAJOR PEACOCK 9th R Inniskilling Fusiliers took command of the Battalion at the CRUCIFIX.	
8.35 p.m.	LIEUT BENNETT 14th, surviving officer of THIEPVAL WOOD 11.15 p.m. the Division has returned with the Battalion & reported that Remainder of Battalion was posted in WHITCHURCH STREET ready for	
2nd July 2.15. 6 a.m.	GERMAN Counter attack.	

Army Form C. 2118.

WAR DIARY
or
INTELLIGENCE SUMMARY.
(Erase heading not required.)

Instructions regarding War Diaries and Intelligence Summaries are contained in F. S. Regs., Part II., and the Staff Manual respectively. Title pages will be prepared in manuscript.

Hour, Date, Place	Summary of Events and Information	Remarks and references to Appendices

2 July 1916.
THIEPVAL WOOD.
 	
1.30 a.m.
	All that remained of Battalion on morning of 2 July; exclusive of Batt. H.Qrs was 2 Officers, 1 Coy S.M. 3 Sgts. & 3 Other Ranks.
	
	A composite Battalion of the Brigade was formed at 2.15 pm again crossed over to the German B. line trenches. The Battalion held this line from A.15 – A.17 until early in the morning of 3rd July. Lieut Bennet in command. During this time the Battalion was heavily shelled & attacked by bombing parties which were all repulsed.
	
	Battalion was relieved from the German line on the morning of 3 July 1916.
	
	The following Officers are mentioned by Major Goodwin for gallant conduct.
	
	    Capt A. FULLERTON. RAMC. (attached)
	    " J.E. SUGDEN. (Adjutant)
	    Lieut A. McCLINTON.
	    " T. BENNET.
	    " A. COLLINGS. (wounded)
	    " M. ADAMSON. (Killed)
	    " STEVENSON. (Wounded)
	    " MASTERMAN. (Killed)
	    Capt BARRY HILL (wounded & missing)	

Army Form C. 2118.

WAR DIARY
or
INTELLIGENCE SUMMARY.
(Erase heading not required.)

10ᵗʰ R.I.R.

Hour, Date, Place	Summary of Events and Information	Remarks and references to Appendices
1 July 1916	The following Officer Casualties occurred in the action from 1st to 3rd July 1916.	
	Killed in Action	
	Colonel. BERNARD. H.C. Commanding.	
	2 Lieut. DEANE. W.	
	" " MASTERMAN. F.M.	
	" " WILSON. E.M.	
	" " ADAMSON. M.L.	
3	" " CRAIG. C.F.	
3	" " CORBETT. D.B.	
	WOUNDED	
1 July 1916.	Capt. GLENDENNING. H.	
	" HILL. B. &(missing)	
	" LANGTRY. W.R.	
	Lieut. COLLINS. A.	
	" WALLACE. A.	
	" JORDAN.	
2	" GREEN. W.O. (believed killed)	
	" CROCKETT.	
	" ELLIOTT. T.B. (believed killed)	
	" STEVENSON. S-J	
	" TOOLEY. F.S.	
3	" CULLEN. F.M.	

10R/12

WAR DIARY
or
INTELLIGENCE SUMMARY.
(Erase heading not required.)

Army Form C. 2118.

Instructions regarding War Diaries and Intelligence Summaries are contained in F. S. Regs., Part II., and the Staff Manual respectively. Title pages will be prepared in manuscript.

Hour, Date, Place	Summary of Events and Information	Remarks and references to Appendices
THIEPVAL WOOD. 2 July 1916.	Relieved by 49th Division in trenches & proceeded to billets in MARTINSART.	
MARTINSART. 4-7-16.	Marched to billets in HARPONVILLE.	
HARPONVILLE. 5-7-16.		
10.7.16.	— — — RUBEMPRÉ	
11.7.16.	— — — BERNAVILLE	
	— — — AUXI LE CHATEAUX.	
AUXI LE CHATEAUX. 11.7.16	Entrained for THIENNE.	
12-7-16.	Marched from THIENNE to WARDREQUES.	
13-7-16.	— " NORTLEULINGHEM, & rest there till 20.7.16.	
20-7-16	Marched to VOLKERINCKHOVE.	
21-7-16	— — WORMHOUDT. (RIETVELD)	
22-7-16.	— — HONDEGHEM.	
23-7-16	— — STEENWERCKEN.	
27-7-16	— — KORTEPYP.	
31-7-16.	— — Neuve Église	
	Took over right of divisional line S.W. of MESSINES in conjunction with 9th R.Ir.Rif: with whom we formed a composite Battalion.	

WAR DIARY
or
INTELLIGENCE SUMMARY.
(Erase heading not required.)

Army Form C. 2118.

10th R.I.R.

Hour, Date, Place	Summary of Events and Information	Remarks and references to Appendices
July 1916.	The following officers joined this Battalion for duty.	
4.7.16.	MAJOR N.G. BURNAND. to command from LEINSTER REGT & 8 R.Irish Rifles	
13.7.16.	2 Lieut. DOYLE. C.S. R. Irish Regt.	
16.7.16.	CAPT. TAYLOR. C. R. Irish Regt	
16.7.16.	O'BEIRNE. C.B. R. Irish Regt	
16.7.16.	2 LIEUT. CAVE. W.F. R. Irish Regt	
16.7.16.	LYTTON. P.A. R. Irish Regt	
16.7.16.	MacLEAN. P.E. R. Irish Regt	
16.7.16.	NOLAN. M.H.W.P. R. Irish Regt	
16.7.16.	HANRATTY. P.A. R. Irish Regt	
16.7.16.	McLEAN. A.H. R. Irish Regt	
22.7.16.	LIEUT. WORKMAN. A.C. R. Irish Regt	
22.7.16.	CAPT. McDONNEL. J.A. R. Irish Rifles	
24.7.16.	2 LIEUT. HARTY. J.J. R. Munster Fus.	
24.7.16.	LIEUT. HACKETT. L.A.H. R. Munster Fus.	
25.7.16.	2 LIEUT. O'ROURKE. G.S. Leinster Regt	
25.7.16.	GRAY. M. R. Dublin Fus.	
25.7.16.	WALKER. A.E. R. Dublin Fus.	
25.7.16.	DALLAGHAN. S.P. Leinster Regt	
		N.G. Burnand Major Comdg: 10 R. Irish Rifles 31-7-16

WAR DIARY
or
INTELLIGENCE SUMMARY
(Erase heading not required.)

Army Form C. 2118

16 D.A.G.
vol. 11

Place	Date	Hour	Summary of Events and Information	Remarks and references to Appendices
LA PLUS DOUVE FM	August 1916. 1st		In trenches with Headquarters at La Plus Douve Farm.	
near BULLE EGLISE NEUVE	5th		Were relieved by 12 & 13 Bn. R. Irish Rifles (108th Bde) & marched to rest billets at LYLO FARM. near Neuve Eglise. Companies being billeted in farms in vicinity.	
	7th		Reinforcements of 30 other Ranks arrived.	
	8th		" " 90 " " "	
	8th		Relieved 9th Bn. R. Irish Rifles in the trenches. Headquarters at St. Quentin Cabt.	
	15th		Reinforcements of 10 other Ranks arrived.	
	16th		Relieved by 9th R. Irish Rifles in trenches & proceeded to KORTEPYP CAMP in Brigade Reserve.	
			Officers reinforcements arrived	
	8th		2nd Lieut. DAVIDSON. J.A.G.	
			" CRAIG. E.E.	
	17th Aug		" HENDERSON. J.O.	

Army Form C. 2118

WAR DIARY
or
INTELLIGENCE SUMMARY
(Erase heading not required.)

10 R. I. Rif.

Place	Date	Hour	Summary of Events and Information	Remarks and references to Appendices
ST QUENTIN CABARET	24 August		Relieved 9th Bn. R Irish Rifles at 5' in trenches in left Sector of Division. Headquarters at St Quentin Cabaret.	
	27.		Draft of 6 Other ranks arrived.	

W.E. Bernard Lt Col
Comdg: 10 R. Irish Rifles
1-9-16

WAR DIARY
or
INTELLIGENCE SUMMARY
(Erase heading not required.)

Army Form C. 2118

10⁰ 12108
Vol 12

Place	Date	Hour	Summary of Events and Information	Remarks and references to Appendices
TRENCHES	1916 1 Sept		Relieved at ST QUENTIN'S CABARET by 9th Bn. R. IRISH RIFLES & proceeded to rest billets at LYLO FARM & vicinity.	
	9 Sept		Relieved the 9th R. IRISH RIFLES in the above named Trenches.	
	17 Sept		Relieved by 9th R. IRISH RIFLES and proceeded into Divisional Reserve at KORTE PYP. CAMP.	
	23 Sept		Relieved the 9th R. IRISH Rifles in the trenches. Two Officers reinforcements arrived from the base.	
	12 Sept			
	29 Sept		Relieved by 9th R. Irish Rifles & proceeded to Brigade Reserve with Headquarters at NEUVE EGLISE.	

W.S. Bunnend Lt/Col
Comdg: 10th R. Ir. Rifles
30. 9. 16

WAR DIARY
INTELLIGENCE SUMMARY
(Erase heading not required.)

Army Form C. 2118

Place	Date 1916	Hour	Summary of Events and Information	Remarks and references to Appendices
NEUVE EGLISE.	27th Sept	11:30 p.m.	Capt & Adjt J.E. SUGDEN D.S.O. was killed in our front line trenches by chance bullet. Buried at St QUENTIN'S CABARET Military Cemetery.	
	October 5th		Relieved 9th Bn. R. Irish Rifles in the trenches.	
	3rd		No. 10/16093 Actg C.S.M. R. WHELAN granted Military Medal.	
	9th		Lieutenant A. COLLINGS ⎫ awarded Military Cross.	
			—"— A.N. McCLINTON. ⎭	
	8/9		Gas attack & raid on enemy trenches 1 mile W of MESSINES. Raiding party. 2nd Lt T.S. HASLETT. ⎫	
			—"— J.A.G. DAVIDSON ⎭ 15 O. ranks. entered enemy trenches, shot enemy, captured 3 Germans two officers wore Iron Crosses, bombed dug outs & returned. 2nd Lt DAVIDSON missing. 2 R.fm. wounded.	
			2nd Lieut T.S. HASLETT. awarded Military Cross.	
	23		Relieved by 9th R. Irish Rifles & proceeded to Divisional Reserve at KORTEPYP CAMP.	
	11th		Relieved 9th R. Irish Rifles in the trenches.	
	17th		—"— —"— & proceeded to B.73rd Reserve at NEUVE EGLISE.	
	23rd		—"— —"—	
	29		Relieved 9th R. Irish Rifles in the trenches.	
	28		Draft of 14 O.R. arrived out on 30th another 28 O.R. arrived.	
	31		B officers Reinforcement arrived.	

Wyndowmand Lt. Col.
COMMDG. 10th ROYAL IRISH RIFLES.

10th Bn R. I. Rifles
Army Form C. 2118

Vol 14

WAR DIARY
or
INTELLIGENCE SUMMARY
(Erase heading not required.)

Place	Date	Hour	Summary of Events and Information	Remarks and references to Appendices
NEUVE EGLISE.	Nov 1916. 4.		Relieved in Trenches by 9th R. Irish Rifles at ST QUENTIN'S CABT. & proceeded to Divisional Reserve in KORTEPYP CAMP.	
	10.	10.15	Relieved 9th R. Irish Rifles in above trenches.	
		16.45	" by " " and proceeded to Brigade Reserve at NEUVE EGLISE.	
	15.		Military Medals were awarded to undermentioned NCOs & men on 15 Nov. 16 for distinguished services performed prior to 1st July 1916.	
			10/14335 2/Cpl: E. Crowe. 'C' Coy	
			6/10504 2/Sgt. J. Meaney 'A'	
			17/1823 Rfm. H. Hodges. "A"	
			10/14186 " R.J. Carson "B"	
			10/15079 2/Sgt W. Kinghorn. "C"	
			10/15383 2/Cpl W. McCrea "C"	
			10/15172 " J. Lough "A"	
			10/15700 " J. Nutt "A"	
			10/14197 Rfm. W. Cathcart. "C"	
			10/16709 L/Cpl W. McCullough. "C"	
			10/13660. Rfm. W. Stevenson. "B"	
	27. 28		Relieved 9th A. IRISH RIFLES in the trenches.	
			" by " " & proceeded to Divisional Reserve at KORTEPYP. CAMP. (OVER)	

Army Form C. 2118

WAR DIARY
or
INTELLIGENCE SUMMARY
(Erase heading not required.)

Place	Date	Hour	Summary of Events and Information	Remarks and references to Appendices
On Service	1916 Nov		Drafts during November 916, arrived as under.	
	1		1 Other rank from Base	
	14		2 " " "	
	17		1 " " "	
	20		70 " " " attached from 1/17 London Regt (T)	
	21		20 " " "	
	27.		17 " " "	
			111 Total.	

[signature]
COMMDG. 18th ROYAL IRISH RIFLES.

WAR DIARY
or
INTELLIGENCE SUMMARY 10th Bn R.Ir. Rifles

Army Form C. 2118

Vol /5

Place	Date	Hour	Summary of Events and Information	Remarks and references to Appendices
On Service	1/2/16		Relieved the 9th Batten R.Ir.Rif. in the trenches at St Quentin Cabt.	
	10/2/16		Relieved by the 9th Batten R.Ir.Rif. at St Quentin Cabt and proceeded into Brigade Reserve at Maukhill Huts.	
	16/2/16		Relieved the 9th Batten R.Ir.Rif in the trenches at St Quentin Cabt.	
	29/2/16		Relieved by the 9th Batten R.Ir.Rif at St Quentin Cabt and proceeded into Divisional Reserve at Wakefield Camp.	
	28/3/16		Relieved the 7th Batten R.Ir.Rif. in the trenches at St Quentin Cabt.	
	2/4/16		Major W.J. Goodwin assumed command of R.I.R.Rif.	
	2/12/16		Capt. Y.N. McCluskin assumed the duties of 2nd in command + T.N.L.	
	8/12/16		2nd Lt. H.W.P. Logan 10th R.I.R. wounded	
	10/12/16		Lieut Col. W.L. Burland assumed temporary command	
	10/12/16		Capt. Y.N. McCluskin assumed command of No Baths Boys	
	10/12/16		Capt. Y.N. Clendon assumed temporary command	
	28/12/16		Lt. J.H. Haskell assumed temporary command of E Company	
	10/12/16		Lt. Y.N. Lanvin assumed temporary command of D Company	
	13/12/16		Lt. De Wetter assumed temporary command of B Company	
	29/12/16		Capt. Debyrne 10th Bn Ox. Covoy of N.451. Wales Bordr	
	30/12/16		Capt. C. Taylor transfered to hospital & sick to C 6 Bath Sight R Regt	

Army Form C. 2118

WAR DIARY
or
INTELLIGENCE SUMMARY

10th Bn. R. Ir. Rifles

(Erase heading not required.)

Instructions regarding War Diaries and Intelligence Summaries are contained in F. S. Regs., Part II. and the Staff Manual respectively. Title Pages will be prepared in manuscript.

Place	Date	Hour	Summary of Events and Information	Remarks and references to Appendices
On Service	5/12/16		The following reinforcements arrived from the Base Depot.	
	13/12/16		14 other ranks	
	14/12/16		3 " "	
	18/12/16		9 " "	
	21/12/16		1 " "	
	22/12/16		2 " "	

F.H. McCluskey Capt.
Commanding 10th R.I.R. Rif.

WAR DIARY or INTELLIGENCE SUMMARY

Army Form C. 2118

1st R.L. Rifles (?)

Place	Date	Hour	Summary of Events and Information	Remarks and references to Appendices
In the Field	3/1/17		Batt'n relieved by the 9th R.I.R. Rgt. in the trenches at St Quentin Cabaret and proceeded into Brigade Reserve at Sharkill Huts	
"	9/1/17		Relieved the 9th Battn. R.I.R. Rgt. in the trenches at St Quentin Cabaret	
"	15/1/17		Relieved in the trenches by the 9th R.I.R. Rgt. and proceeded into Divisional Reserve at KORTEPYP CAMP.	
"	21/1/17		Relieved the 9th R.I.R. Rgt. in the trenches at St Quentin Cabaret	
"	27/1/17		Relieved in the trenches at St Quentin Cabaret by the 12th R.I.R. Rgt. and proceeded into rest billets at BULFORD CAMP	
			Awards	
			Capt. A. Fletcher R.A.M.C. attached 10th R.I.R. awarded the Military Cross in the new Letters	
	3/1/17		of Honours.	
			Mentioned in Despatches	
			Lt. & Capt. T.M. Knoth	
			Lt. J.H. Lugden D.S.O.	
			No 18143 C.S.M. Davison T.	
	5/1/17		Reinforcement 14339 Pte J Wardle &	
	13/1/17		Lt. & Capt. T. Rod from Base Depot	
	16/1/17		3 other ranks from Base Depot	do
			do	do

WAR DIARY
or
INTELLIGENCE SUMMARY

Army Form C. 2118

Place	Date	Hour	Summary of Events and Information	Remarks and references to Appendices
In the Field	24/11/17		Reinforcement continued to join unit from Base Depot	
	17/11/17		" " " " " 9th Batln R.I.R.	
	20/11/17		" " " " " 32nd Bn R.A.	
	20/11/17		" " " " " Base Depot	
	25/11/17		2 " " " " 9 R.I.R.	
	28/11/17		1 " " " " Journeyed Reg or Cy	
	28/11/17		1 Officer from Base Depot 2nd Lt E.B. Fallows	
	28/11/17		1 Officer from Base Train Bays J. Cepts	
	10/11/17		1 Officer from Base Depot 2nd Lt H. Atkinson	

W. W. Crichton Capt.
Comdg 10th R.I.R.

Army Form C. 2118.

10 R Irish Rifles

Vol 17

WAR DIARY
or
INTELLIGENCE SUMMARY.
(Erase heading not required.)

Instructions regarding War Diaries and Intelligence Summaries are contained in F.S. Regs., Part II. and the Staff Manual respectively. Title pages will be prepared in manuscript.

Place	Date	Hour	Summary of Events and Information	Remarks and references to Appendices
NEUVE EGLISE	1917			
BULFORD CAMP.	4 Feb		Draft of 144 OtherRanks transferred to this Battalion from 7 & 13ᵗʰ Essex Regt.	
"	7 Feb		" 82 " " from Base Depot.	
"	11 "		Lieut. A. WALLACE arrived from " "	
"	17 "		Draft of 44 Other Ranks from Base Depot.	
"	19 "		The Battalion moved to PINCH BOOM near METEREN.	
PINCHBOOM. 26 "			RED LODGE (BOUVE AREA) in Brigade Reserve.	
RED LODGE. 27 "			2 Lieut F.S. TOOLEY arrived from Base depot.	

N.E. Bernard. Lt.Col.
Comdg: 10 R. Irish. Rifles.
28. 2. 17.

Army Form C. 2118.

WAR DIARY
or
INTELLIGENCE SUMMARY. 10th R. Irish Rifles
(Erase heading not required.)

Vol 18

Place	Date	Hour	Summary of Events and Information	Remarks and references to Appendices
LA DOUVE SECTOR	1/3/17		The Batt. relieved the 9th Battn Royal Irish Rifles in the trenches.	
"	5/3/17		1 other rank killed.	
"	7/3/17		1 other rank wounded.	
			The Batt. was relieved in the trenches by the 9th R. Irish Rifles, and went to Brigade Reserve at RED LODGE.	
RED LODGE	9/3/17		1 other rank wounded.	
"	12/3/17		The Batt. marched to KEMMEL and relieved the 6th Battn Connaught Rangers in Brigade Support (47 Inf. Bde.)	
KEMMEL SECTOR	13/3/17		The Batt. relieved the 6th Battn. Royal Irish Regiment in the trenches.	
"	16/3/17		3 other ranks wounded.	
"	17/3/17		9 officers & reinforcements arrived from BASE DEPOT.	
"	18/3/17		1 other rank wounded.	
"	19/3/17		1 officer transferred to, and 1 officer attached to, the 15th Royal Irish Rifles.	
"	20/3/17		The Batt. was relieved by the 9th Royal Irish Rifles, and went to Brigade Reserve at DERRY HUTS	
DERRY HUTS	21/3/17		1 officer and 11 other ranks reinforcements arrived from BASE DEPOT	
"	24/3/17		Batt. shelled in huts. 2nd Lt. J.W. KNOX & 4 other ranks wounded.	
			Summer time introduced at 11 p.m.	
KEMMEL SECTOR	25/3/17		The Batt. relieved the 9th Royal Irish Rifles in the trenches:	

Army Form C. 2118.

WAR DIARY
or
INTELLIGENCE SUMMARY.
(Erase heading not required.)

Place	Date	Hour	Summary of Events and Information	Remarks and references to Appendices
KEMMEL SECTOR	29/3/17		1 officer and 10 other ranks reinforcements arrived from BASE DEPOT.	N.E. Drummond Lt Col. Comdg: 10 R. Irish Rif. Rs. 1 – 4 – 17.
"	31/3/17		Batt. was relieved in the trenches by the 9th R.I. Rifles and went into Brigade Support in KEMMEL	

Army Form C. 2118.

10th R. Irish Rifles
Vol 19

WAR DIARY
~~INTELLIGENCE~~ SUMMARY.
(Erase heading not required)

Instructions regarding War Diaries and Intelligence Summaries are contained in F. S. Regs., Part II. and the Staff Manual respectively. Title pages will be prepared in manuscript.

Place	Date	Hour	Summary of Events and Information	Remarks and references to Appendices
KEMMEL	1.4.17		8 other ranks arrived from BASE DEPOT	
"	7.4.17		The Battalion went into DIVISIONAL SUPPORT at WAKEFIELD HUTS.	
WAKEFIELD HUTS	8.4.17		1 OFFICER arrived from BASE DEPOT.	
"	13.4.17		13 other ranks arrived from BASE DEPOT.	
"	15.4.17		Battalion commenced march to BOUVELINGHEM TRAINING Area. Billeted for night at HAZEBROUCK.	
HAZEBROUCK	16.4.17		Battalion marched from HAZEBROUCK to ARQUES. Billeted at ARQUES for the night.	
ARQUES	17.4.17		Battalion marched from ARQUES to TRAINING AREA. Billeted in MORNINGHEM.	
MORNINGHEM	22.4.17		4 other ranks arrived from BASE DEPOT.	
"	30.4.17		Battalion commenced march to METEREN AREA. Billeted at ARQUES for the night. 2nd Lieut J.H. CORDNER and 2 other ranks proceeded to HAVRE. as instructors at CENTRAL TRAINING SCHOOL.	

Strength of Battalion on last day of this month.
39 Officers. 884 other Ranks.

W.G. Bernard Lt Col.
Comdg 10 R. Irish Rifles
30.4.-17

Army Form C. 2118.

WAR DIARY
or
INTELLIGENCE SUMMARY

(Erase heading not required.) 10th Bn. The Royal Irish Rifles.

Instructions regarding War Diaries and Intelligence Summaries are contained in F. S. Regs., Part II. and the Staff Manual respectively. Title pages will be prepared in manuscript.

Place	Date	Hour	Summary of Events and Information	Remarks and references to Appendices
ARQUES	1.5.17		Battalion marched from ARQUES to HAZEBROUCK, on return from leaving area.	
HAZEBROUCK	2.5.17		Battalion marched from HAZEBROUCK to METEREN area.	
METEREN	3.5.17		8 other ranks reinforcements arrived from BASE DEPOT	
"	5.5.17		1 Officer reinforcement arrived from BASE DEPOT.	
"	13.5.17		1 officer and 4 other ranks reinforcements arrived from BASE DEPOT.	
"	14.5.17		Battalion marched to new Bryant area – BAILLEUL – DRANOUTRE (MILLE)	
MILLE	16.5.17		41 other ranks reinforcements arrived from BASE DEPOT.	
"	17.5.17		1 Officer reinforcement arrived from BASE DEPOT.	
"	18.5.17		7 other ranks reinforcements arrived from BASE DEPOT.	
"	19.5.17		16 other ranks reinforcements arrived from BASE DEPOT.	
"	21.5.17		1 officer and 50 other ranks reinforcements arrived from BASE DEPOT.	
"	24.5.17		18 other ranks reinforcements arrived from BASE DEPOT.	
"	25.5.17		Lieut-Col N.G. BURNARD, Lieut and Quartermast. C.H.T. DAWSON, No.9/945 Sergt. SHAW and No. 15388 Sergt. A. McCUNE mentioned in despatches. London Gazette 25 May 1917	
"	26.5.17		20 other ranks reinforcements arrived from BASE DEPOT.	
"	27.5.17		1 other rank wounded	
"	28.5.17		1 other rank wounded	
"	29.5.17		248 other ranks reinforcements arrived from BASE DEPOT (attached to 107th M.G. Company)	
"	30.5.17		1 other rank wounded. Battalion moved to BERTHEN area.	
			Strength (31.5.17) — 43 officers and 1007 other ranks	

M Stewart
Lieut. Col.
Comdg. 10th Royal Irish Rifles.

Army Form C. 2118.

10/3 b

WAR DIARY
or
INTELLIGENCE SUMMARY.

(Erase heading not required.) 1/6 (S) Bn. The Royal Irish Rifles

Vol 21

Instructions regarding War Diaries and Intelligence Summaries are contained in F. S. Regs., Part II. and the Staff Manual respectively. Title pages will be prepared in manuscript.

Place	Date	Hour	Summary of Events and Information	Remarks and references to Appendices
BERTHEN	1.6.17		1 O.r. wounded.	
"	5.6.17		1 Officer reinforcement arrived from BASE DEPOT.	
"	6.6.17		1 Officer and 1 O.r. reinforcement arrived from BASE DEPOT.	
"	6.6.17		Battalion marched to HILLE CAMP, and from there into action.	
MESSINES	7.6.17		Attack on MESSINES RIDGE. Total Casualties 1 Officer killed and 2 wounded. 9 O.r. killed and 50 wounded. 2 O.r. missing. Full Story attached.	
WYTSCHAETE RIDGE				
HILLE	9.6.17		Battalion marched to HILLE Camp.	
"	12.6.17		11 O.r. reinforcements arrived from BASE DEPOT.	
"	13.6.17		Battalion marched to area 13 (outside BAILLEUL)	
BAILLEUL	18.6.17		Battalion marched to KEMMEL HILL.	
WYTSCHAETE	19.6.17		Battalion relieved 5th DORSETS in support line.	
"	21.6.17		1 O.r. wounded.	
OOSTTAVERNE	24.6.17		Battalion relieved 9th R. Ir. Rif. in front line. 1 O.r. wounded.	
"	22.6.17		1 Officer reinforcement arrived.	
"	25.6.17		1 O.r. killed 4 O.r. wounded.	

Army Form C. 2118.

WAR DIARY
or
INTELLIGENCE SUMMARY.
(Erase heading not required.)

10th (S) Bn The Royal Irish Rifles

Instructions regarding War Diaries and Intelligence Summaries are contained in F. S. Regs., Part II. and the Staff Manual respectively. Title pages will be prepared in manuscript.

Place	Date	Hour	Summary of Events and Information	Remarks and references to Appendices
OOSTAVERNE	26.6.17		7 O.T. Killed S O.T. wounded	
	27.6.17		5 O.T. wounded	
	28.6.17		4 O.T. killed S O.T. wounded	
			Battalion relieved by 13th K.R.R. and marched to LOCRE.	
LOCRE	30.6.17		Battalion marched to MERRIS area	

HCLindwing Capt
Comdg. 10th R.I.R.

WAR DIARY
or
INTELLIGENCE SUMMARY
(Erase heading not required.)

Army Form C. 2118.

10(S) Bn. The Royal Irish Rifles.

Place	Date	Hour	Summary of Events and Information	Remarks and references to Appendices
opposite MESSINES Ridge.	7.6.17	3.10 a.m.	The attack on the MESSINES ridge commenced. The primary object was the taking of Messines, and the 36th Division was allotted the Centre portion between MESSINES & WYTSCHAETE, with the 25th Division on its right, and the 16th Division on its left. The 107th & 109th Brigades of the 36th Div. were in the assaulting waves, whilst the 108th Bde was in Divn reserve. The 10th R.Ir.Rif. was the left Batln of the 107th Bde and was in Bde reserve. Order of Battle :- On the Brigade right the 8th R.Ir.Rif. " " " " left " 9th R.Ir.Rif. " " " Bde reserve right 15th R.Ir.Rif. " " " " left " 10th R.Ir.Rif. The left flank of the Batln was on the Northernmost portion of the hill called SPANBROEKMOLEN whilst the right flank was some 100 yards south of this point. The direction was practically due East, leaving L'ENFER WOOD on the right of the Batln. The final objective of the Batln was a line running roughly 300 yds East of the MESSINES - WYTSCHAETE ridge. The Batln left its trenches for the assault at 3.10 a.m., two hours after the first assaulting waves had gone over. The Germans appeared to be entirely taken by surprise, and the sudden blowing up of several enormous mines completely stunned them. There mines had	

1577 Wt. W.10791/1773 500,000 1/15 D. D. & L. A.D.S.S./Forms/C. 2118.

WAR DIARY
or
INTELLIGENCE SUMMARY.

(Erase heading not required.) 10th (S) Bn. The Royal Irish Rifles.

Army Form C. 2118.

Place	Date	Hour	Summary of Events and Information	Remarks and references to Appendices
			been done two years in making. Immediately the mines were fired, the first waves rushed over the parapet. Everything went without a hitch. Officers and men were mad for blood, but very few Germans stayed to meet them; though many came in as prisoners, scarcely any showed fight. The order of Battle for the Batt. was, from left to right and from right to left. 1st and 2nd waves A Company — Lieut J.A. COEY B Company — a/Capt J.H. STEWART 3rd and 4th waves C Company — Lieut L.A.H. HACKETT D Company — Lieut R. McLAURIN (killed) Little opposition was shown until the vicinity of the MESSINES – WYTSCHAETE road was reached, by which time C and D Companies had passed through A and B Companies and were moving to the final objective. C Company's objective, a road running 400 yds East of the MESSINES-WYTSCHAETE road, was strongly held by German machine guns. Several machine guns opened fire on C and D Companies at this point, and a combined attack by these companies was organised. Lieut R. McLAURIN was hit, killed, and 2nd Lieut H. ROSS and 2nd Lieut J. MARTIN wounded. No 16/12759 Sergt D. IRWIN was killed, and several other casualties sustained. 2nd Lieut G.Y. HENDERSON accounted for one enemy machine gun, by stalking three crews his on it with rifle grenades.	

WAR DIARY
or
INTELLIGENCE SUMMARY

(Erase heading not required.) 10th (S) Bn. The Royal Irish Rifles.

Army Form C. 2118.

Place	Date	Hour	Summary of Events and Information	Remarks and references to Appendices

Whilst No.6/16093 C.S.M. R.S. WHELAN, firing a previously captured strong point, opened fire with a captured enemy machine gun, and enabled the flanking parties to work round the flanks, assisted by our own Lewis gun fire. A tank also co-operated in this enterprise. On finding their flanks threatened, the enemy displayed the white flag and surrendered. The "bag" comprised one Regimental Commander, thirty other officers and seventy men, who were taken prisoner, and four machine guns. A patrol under No. 10/16093 C.S.M. R.S. WHELAN and No.6/1166 Sergt. T. PATTON then went forward and captured an enemy reconnoitring patrol of one officer and thirty men, also a field gun a little further on.

The Battn. then proceeded to consolidate its position, and was relieved by another battalion of the Divn. at 2 a.m. The Battn. then marched back about 1½ miles, where it rested during the 8th of June. The numbers who actually took part in the assault on the 7th of June were:—

Officers 25
Other Ranks 532

The remainder of the Battn. was left behind to form a nucleus of specialists etc., in the event of heavy casualties. The total casualties for the 7th of June were:—

Army Form C. 2118.

WAR DIARY
or
INTELLIGENCE SUMMARY.

(Erase heading not required.) 10th (S) Bn. The Royal Irish Rifles

Place	Date	Hour	Summary of Events and Information	Remarks and references to Appendices
			Killed. Wounded. Missing.	
			Officers. 1 2 0	
			Other ranks. 7 49 5	

Army Form C. 2118.

WAR DIARY
or
INTELLIGENCE SUMMARY.
(Erase heading not required.) 1st (S) Bn. The Royal Irish Rifles.

Vol 22

Place	Date	Hour	Summary of Events and Information	Remarks and references to Appendices
OUTTERSTEEN	1.7.17		5 other ranks reinforcements arrived from BASE DEPOT.	
"	5.7.17		Battalion marched to CAESTRE area, en route to training area.	
CAESTRE	6.7.17		Battalion marched to RENESCURE area.	
RENESCURE	7.7.17		Battalion marched to LE POUVRE, in TILQUES training area for training.	
LE POUVRE	8.7.17		Military Medal awarded to No 10/16686 Rfm LUCAS J and No 10/14311 Rfm MINTER F.G.	
"	9.7.17		34 other ranks reinforcements arrived from BASE DEPOT.	
"	12.7.17		Inter-Unit Sports	
"	19.7.17		50 O.Rs reinforcements arrived from Base Depot.	
"	20.7.17		Battalion marched to ESQUERDES and continued training	
"	16.7.17		Military Cross awarded to Lieut. L.A.H. HACKETT 2/Lt G.V. HENDERSON and 10/16597 Sgt E. MILNE C.S.M. R.S. WHELAN. Military Medal awarded to 10/16597 Sgt E. MILNE	
ESQUERDES	25.7.17		Battalion embussed at SETQUES and proceeded to WINIZEELE area	
OUDEZEELE	26.7.17		6 O.Rs reinforcements arrived from BASE DEPOT.	
"	30.7.17		Battalion marched to WATOU No 3 AREA at 10 p.m. and became part of Corps Reserve to which 36th Divn. was allotted for the coming offensive.	
"	31.7.17		Strength — Officers 41 O.R. 921	

Whitmarsh, Lieut Col D.S.O.
Comdg 10th (S) Bn The Royal Irish Rifles

WAR DIARY or INTELLIGENCE SUMMARY

Army Form C. 2118.

107/36 10th R. Irish Rifles

3rd Battle of YPRES.

Place	Date	Hour	Summary of Events and Information	Remarks
WATOU	1917 2nd Aug		Entrained E. of POPERINGHE for DEAD END. Thence marched to take over trenches from 6th Connaught Rangers with B" Hqrs in VINERY. Night of 2/3rd relieved 55th Div" in WIELTJE sector of Black line. Hqrs at PLUM F". Trenches very wet and hostile shelling considerable.	
PLUM F"	5th Aug		Relieved by 9th R.I. Rif and took over BLUE Line with Hqrs at UHLAN F". Same conditions as in BLACK LINE. Ration parties however had not so far to carry. Battalion now in Brigade Reserve.	
UHLAN F"	6th Aug 7th Aug		A and D Coys withdrawn to old BRITISH FRONT LINE at night between WARWICK CASTLE & WIELTJE. Relieved by 12th R.I. Rif and marched to RED ROSE CAMP. W. of VLAMERTINGHE. Casualties during phase – Cap" M? Forbes gassed – 112 O.R.s by Artillery. Casualties mostly taken by ration parties & stretcher bearers.	
VLAMERTINGHE	12th Aug		Having rested and re-equipped, Batt" relieved 12th R.I. Rif in PLUM F" having proceeded by train to DEAD END.	
" "				
PLUM F"	14th Aug 15th Aug		Relieved by 13th R.I. Rif and 9th R.I. Ins. and trained from DEAD END to RED ROSE CAMP.	
VLAMERTINGHE	16th Aug	2 A.M.	Proceeded by train to DEAD END and went into trenches with VINERY as Batt" Hqrs. Batt" part of Divisional Reserve for offensive on 16th/17th Aug.	
VINERY	18th Aug		Relieved by 61st Division and went into camp S.E. of VLAMERTINGHE.	
VLAMERTINGHE	20th Aug		Entrained and proceeded to OUDEZEELE	
OUDEZEELE	" "		Entrained at ESPEULBECQ, detrained BAPAUME en route to IVth Corps (5th Army) and marched to camp in BARASTRE	

Army Form C. 2118.

WAR DIARY
or
INTELLIGENCE SUMMARY.
(Erase heading not required.)

Instructions regarding War Diaries and Intelligence Summaries are contained in F. S. Regs., Part II. and the Staff Manual respectively. Title pages will be prepared in manuscript.

Place	Date	Hour	Summary of Events and Information	Remarks and references to Appendices
	1917			
BARASTRE	27th		Marched to camp S. of YTRES.	
YTRES	28		Entrained at YTRES and proceeded to take over line from 4th Regt S. AFRICAN Bde in TRESCAULT	
			Left Sub-sector. Trenches very good. Activity practically nil. Batt Hdqrs in TRESCAULT.	
	29.		Reinforcements of 213 O.R. from 8/9th Rt. Rif on amalgamation —	
	31.		Strength of Battalion.	
			Officers 40	
			O Ranks 957.	

R.E. Beauvoir Lt.Col. sdo
Comdg 8th Rt Rif.

1-9-17.

WAR DIARY
of
INTELLIGENCE SUMMARY.
(Erase heading not required.)

Army Form C. 2118.

Place	Date 1917	Hour	Summary of Events and Information	Remarks and references to Appendices
TRESCAULT sector	Sept 3rd		Battalion relieved in the line by 8th/9th R.S. Rif and 1st R.S. Fus and	
EQUANCOURT	8th		withdrawn into Divisional Reserve in EQUANCOURT.	
	9th		3 O.Rs transferred to 233" Employment Coy.	
TRESCAULT	15th		Battn relieved 1st R.S. Fus in the line	
METZ	20th		Relieved by 1st R.S. Fus and withdrawn to Brigade Reserve in METZ.	
—	21		16 O.Rs reinforcements at 36th Div. Depot Battn	
—	21		— " — " — " — " — in line.	
TRASCAULT	26		Relieved 1st R.S. Fus in line.	
	27		1 Officer (Capt. M. FORBES) and 32 O.Rs reported at 36th Div Depot Battn	
EQUANCOURT	30		Relieved by 1st R.S. Fus and withdrawn to Divisional Reserve in EQUANCOURT.	
			3 O.Rs wounded in September.	
			Strength - 39 Officers 963 O.Rs.	

N.F. Burrowes. Lieut. Col.
Comdg. 10th (S) Bn. The Royal Irish Rifles.

WAR DIARY or INTELLIGENCE SUMMARY

Army Form C. 2118.

10th [S] Bn. R. Ir. Rifles

Vol 75

Hour, Date, Place	Summary of Events and Information	Remarks and references to Appendices
October 3rd 1917	The Battn. relieved the 1st Battn. R. Ir. Fusiliers in the trenches (Gavrelle Sector) during this tour number of casualties 1 O.R. wounded.	
October 9th 1917	1 Officer and 7 O.R. raided the enemy outpost line inflicting several casualties and bringing back 1 wounded prisoner belonging to 84th R.I.R. No casualties were sustained by the raiding party. On this date also the Battn. was relieved by the 1st Battn. R. Ir. Fus. and went into Brigade reserve in METZ	
October 15th 1917	Battn. relieved 1st Battn. R. Ir. Fus. in trenches.	
October 21st 1917	Battn. was relieved in trenches by 1st Battn. R. Ir. Fus. and went into Divl. reserve at EROANCOURT.	
October 27th 1917	Battn. relieved 1st Battn. R. Ir. Fus. in trenches.	
October 29th 1917	1 O.R. killed 2 O.R. wounded.	
October 1st – 1917	Reinforcements during October:- 7 Officers from 8/9th R. Ir. Rifles [taken on strength from 29/9/17] October 4th 1917 — 1 Officer at 10th Corps Reinforcement Camp. October 11th 1917 — 10 O.R. from Base Depot through 7th Corps Reinforcement Camp. October 25th 1917 — 3 Officers and 10 O.R. from Base Depot. October 26th 1917 — 1 Officer from 14th R. Ir. Rifles. October 28th 1917 — 1 Officer at 7th Corps Reinforcement Camp. October 31st 1917 — 19 O.R. from 7th Corps Reinforcement Camp.	E.W. Macnaghten Lieut. Col. in Cmd. 10th Rifles

10 R. Irish Rifles.

Vol 26

Army Form C. 2118.

WAR DIARY
or
INTELLIGENCE SUMMARY.
(Erase heading not required.)

Instructions regarding War Diaries and Intelligence Summaries are contained in F. S. Regs., Part II., and the Staff Manual respectively. Title pages will be prepared in manuscript.

Hour, Date, Place	Summary of Events and Information	Remarks and references to Appendices
2 Nov 1917. HAPPINCOURT SECTOR	Battalion was relieved in trenches by 1st R Ir Fus and went to Bde Reserve in METZ.	
3 Nov 1917.	1 Sergt killed 7 O.R. wounded.	
4.6.7 Nov	6 Officer reinforcements arrived from IV Corps Reinforcement Camp	
7 Nov	Battn relieved 1 R. Ir. Fus in trenches	
13	Battn was relieved by 1 R Ir Fus in trenches & went to Divl Res. in VALLULART WOOD.	
13	29 O.R. reinforcements transferred from 11 R. Ir. Rif.	
14	22 " " " from IV Corps Reinforcement Camp.	
15	6 " "	
20	Battn marched to SLAG HEAP S. of HERMIES preparatory to going into action	
	Strength. Officers. O.R.	
	The following officers were returned to remain in rear with the surplus personnel Lieut Col N.G. BROMAND DSO. Lieut T.G. HENDERSON	
	and other ranks	
	All remaining officers & other ranks of the battalion were either employed or detached or temp H.Q. or in or on courses, schools & leave.	
	Total Strength of Battalion on this day was 53 Officers 947 other ranks.	

WAR DIARY
or
INTELLIGENCE SUMMARY.
(Erase heading not required.)

Army Form C. 2118.

Hour, Date, Place	Summary of Events and Information	Remarks and references to Appendices
20th Nov. 1917.	Batt. occupied German Support line N.E. of HAVRINCOURT for night.	Strength of Batt. going into action :- 20 Officers 562 OR's plus Med Officer and Chaplain -
21st Nov. 3 p.m.	Proceeded to HINDENBURG SUPPORT LINE S. of the GRAINCOURT - DEMICOURT ROAD.	Casualties :-
22nd Nov.	Moved up HINDENBURG SUPPORT in rear of 15. R.IR.RIF. who were to clear Trenches N. of CAMBRAI - BAPAUME ROAD as far as CANAL DU NORD when 10th Bn here to pass through them. Progress was stopped by Strong Points before the objective of 15. R.IR.RIF. was reached. During fighting here, Capt. J.C. JAMISON. Lieuts G.Y. HENDERSON, M.C. A. McKEE, T.S. HASLETT, M.C. and 2nd Lieuts Wm. A. SCOTT, T.F. McKAY, and H. ATKINSON here killed and 2nd Lieut GATENSBY wounded.	Officers Killed. 5 Wounded. 1 Missing. 1 } believed Wounded + Missing 1 } killed. Other Ranks Killed. 18. Wounded 69. Missing 10.
23rd Nov.	The Batt. was to support the 89th R.IR.RIF. and 1st R.IR.Fus in a further attack on the objectives of the 22nd inst after the 15th R.IR.RIF. had cleared the Strong Point, with the aid of Tanks. The attack did not however develop as expected, and with the exception that B.Coy. under 2/Lieut S.G. THOMAS advanced to ROUND TRENCH, no progress was made. The Batt. was then ordered to get into touch with the 40th Division on the right. The Batt. was moved into the HINDENBURG SUPPORT LINE S. of the 15th R. IR. RIF.	Strength of Batt. on 30. XI. 17. 47 Officers 854 OR's.
24th. Nov.	Batt. relieved by 1st K.R.R. Corps. and withdrawn to old BRITISH Support Line near HERMIES.	
27th Nov.	- Marched to BARASTRE.	
28th Nov.	- Marched to HERMIES.	
29th Nov.	Entrained at YTRES and proceeded to BERNEVILLE.	
30th Nov.	. Marched to COURCELLES - LE - COMTE.	

10 R Irish Rifle
Vol 27

WAR DIARY

Army Form C. 2118

(Erase heading not required.)

Hour, Date, Place	Summary of Events and Information	Remarks and references to Appendices
BERNEVILLE. December 1st 1917.	Battn. marched from COURCELLES to BEAULENCOURT.	Casualties during Month
2nd	Continued march to LECHELLE and went into hutted camp	2/Lieut F.R. FRANKLIN. Wounded and missing believed killed.
4th	marched to trenches near BEAUCAMP and became part of Brigade in Reserve. Battalion Headquarters in CHARING CROSS. Transport lines and Q.M. Stores at SOREL-LE-GRAND.	2/Lieut HANNA. Wounded
5th – 7th	In trenches near BEAUCAMP. Had frost. Men had very little shelter.	Killed 5 O.R.
8th	Relieved 11th R. INNIS. FUS. in line N. of LA VACQUERIE. 6. O.R. Wounded.	Wounded 32 O.R.
9th	Battn. carried out a minor operation to improve position on WELSH RIDGE.	Missing 1 O.R.
	Consisted of 3 bombing attacks along trenches running toward Enemy lines	Reinforcements
	2/Lieut F.R. FRANKLIN. Wounded and Missing believed Killed. 2/Lieut HANNA	Dec 14th 14 O.R. from Reinforcement Camp
	Wounded. 2 O.R. Killed. 13 O.R. Wounded + O.R. Missing.	22nd 34 O.R. " "
10th	Lt. Col N.G. BURNAND. D.S.O. proceeded to command 109th Inf. Brigade. Major G.M.P.	29th 5 O.R. " "
	HORNIDGE M.C. arrived to command Battalion.	Strength of Battalion on 31st Dec.
12th	Battalion relieved by 15th R.I.R. RIF. and became Brigade Support	46 Officers 989 O Ranks.
13th	Battalion relieved by 3 Coys. 2nd R.I.R. RIF. and 1 Coy 11/13th R.I.R. RIF. and withdrawn	Awarded Military Medal
	to COUILLET WOOD. Less 2 Coys attached 1st R.I.R. FUS. and plus 1 Coy 2nd R.I.R. RIF	10/14186 A/Cpl. R.J. Carson MM (Bar)
	as support to 108th Inf. Bde.	10/15622 Cpl. E. Moore
16th	Relieved by 4th Bedf. Regt. and withdrawn to METZ.	10/14453 A/Cpl. W. Glover
17th	marched to ETRICOURT and spent night in tents.	11/1272 Rfn R.G. Godwin
18th	Entrained ETRICOURT and proceeded to MONDICOURT. marched to	
	GRAND RULLECOURT. Roads almost impassable owing to heavy snow.	C.M. Hornidge Major
	Transport marching by road experienced great difficulty, finally arrived on	Commdg 10th Bn R. Ir. Rifles
21st		
	marched to MONDICOURT and entrained for CORBIE area.	
	Billeted in LA NEUVILLE.	

Army Form C. 2118.

WAR DIARY
or
INTELLIGENCE SUMMARY.
(Erase heading not required)

Instructions regarding War Diaries and Intelligence Summaries are contained in F. S. Regs., Part II. and the Staff Manual respectively. Title pages will be prepared in manuscript.

Place	Date 1918	Hour	Summary of Events and Information	Remarks and references to Appendices
LA NEUVILLE (CORBIE)	Jan. 1–6		Training round ANEUVILLE & preparing to take over from the French.	
	7/8		Marched to MESNIL-ST-NICAISE.	
	9/10		— ,, — ROSIERES	
MESNIL-S:N:	11.		— ,, — to AUBIGNY & BRMY. ST.CHRISTOPHE. Found AUBIGNY occupied by French 30 Inf whole Battn. less 'A' Coy (att. 1 R.I. Fus.) at BRMY. ST.CHRISTOPHE. Back accommodation here so marched to DORE.	
DORE.	12		Marched to GRUGIES at dusk & relieved 2nd Battn 24th French Inf: Regt: in support Posters. A Coy went into the line with 1st R.F. Fus.	
GRUGIES.	18.		Relieved 1st R-Ir Fus in left sub-sector. C. Coy on Right R. on Left. B in Support. A in Reserve	
	21 ST		A & B Coys relieved C & D respectively	
	22 nd		2 Lieut T. F. Scilley & Sergt C. TOWNSEND & Kla brooms whilst on Patrol. 2. O.R. Wounded.	
GRUGIES & CLERMES	23		Battn. less D Coy were relieved in the line by 1 R Ir Fus & went into Brigade Reserve about 1½ miles back.	
	27.		C. Coy relieved D Coy in the trenches.	
	30.		Battn. relieved 1/ R Irish Fus: in the line	
			Reinforcements joining the unit 7.	
	7.		15. O.R. from 16/R. Ir Rif.	
	19.		Africa 10 O.R. from Rif Wing.	
			Strength in Battle De: 31 January 1918. 40 officers 930. O.R.	

Signed R. Good Wyfr
10 R Innis Fus

www.ingramcontent.com/pod-product-compliance
Lightning Source LLC
Chambersburg PA
CBHW081244170426
43191CB00034B/2032